curiousabout
BASEBALL

BY THOMAS K. AND HEATHER ADAMSON

AMICUS

What are you

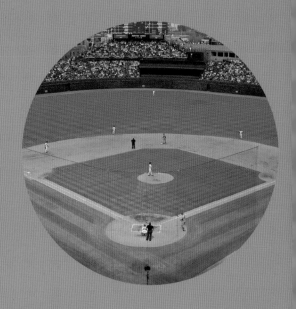

curious about?

CHAPTER **3** THREE

Playing the Game
PAGE
12

Curious About is published by Amicus
P.O. Box 227
Mankato, MN 56002
www.amicuspublishing.us

Editor: Alissa Thielges
Series Designer: Kathleen Petelinsek
Book Designer: Lori Bye
Photo Researcher: Omay Ayres

Library of Congress Cataloging-in-Publication Data
Names: Adamson, Thomas K., 1970- author.
| Adamson, Heather, 1974- author.
Title: Curious about baseball / by Thomas K.
and Heather Adamson.
Description: Mankato, MN: Amicus, [2024] | Series: Curious
about sports | Includes bibliographical references and
index. | Audience: Ages 6–9 | Audience: Grades 2–3 |
Summary: "Conversational questions and answers share what
kids can expect when they join a baseball team. A Stay
Curious! feature models research skills while simple
infographics support visual literacy"—Provided by publisher.
Identifiers: LCCN 2022039970 (print) | LCCN 2022039971
(ebook) | ISBN 9781645493204 (library binding) | ISBN
9781681528441 (paperback) | ISBN 9781645494089 (ebook)
Subjects: LCSH: Baseball—Juvenile literature.
Classification: LCC GV867.5 .A334 2024 (print) | LCC
GV867.5 (ebook) | DDC 796.357—dc23/eng/20220825
LC record available at https://lccn.loc.gov/2022039970
LC ebook record available at https://lccn.loc.gov/2022039971

Photo credits: Alamy/Zoonar GmbH 18; Dreamstime/
Stevendalewhite 9; Getty/Cavan Images 19, LWA 5, Tim Clayton
- Corbis 13, Yoshiyoshi Hirokawa, cover, 1; Shutterstock/Frank
Romeo 6–7, kivnl 8, mayalis 22 and 23 (icons), olllikeballoon
21 (hands), PeopleImages.com - Yuri A 21 (t), Robert J
Daveant 16, Satoshi_Hyodo 14–15, Steve Broer 10–11

Printed in China

CHAPTER ONE

What happens at baseball practice?

You'll learn to catch and throw! You'll also swing a bat to practice hitting. Don't forget to bring a baseball glove. Bring a cap as well to shade your eyes from the sun. Many players wear long pants so they can slide into base.

DID YOU KNOW?

Batters and catchers have safety gear. Batters wear a helmet. Catchers wear a mask and other pads.

Use a glove to catch so you don't hurt your hand.

What are the parts of a baseball field?

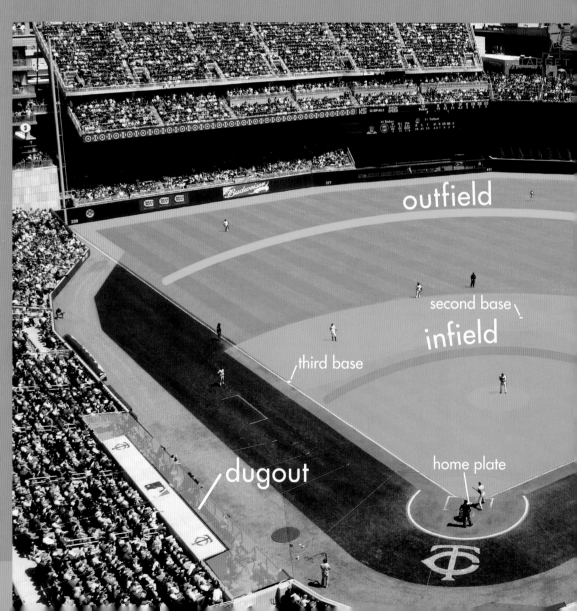

outfield

second base

infield

third base

home plate

dugout

Playing baseball takes a lot of space! The **infield** has three bases and a home plate. Some infields are all dirt. Some have grass. The **outfield** is the grassy space past the bases. When not on the field, players sit in a dugout.

first base

dugout

No matter what level you play at, a baseball field has the same parts.

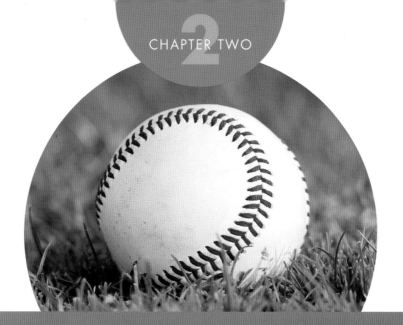

CHAPTER TWO

How do I start playing?

Many kids start with **tee** ball. Some leagues start with coach-pitch. The coach tosses the ball for the batter to hit. The goal is to develop your skills and have fun. Younger kids play on a smaller field. They may also use softer baseballs.

A tee helps players learn how to stand and swing when batting.

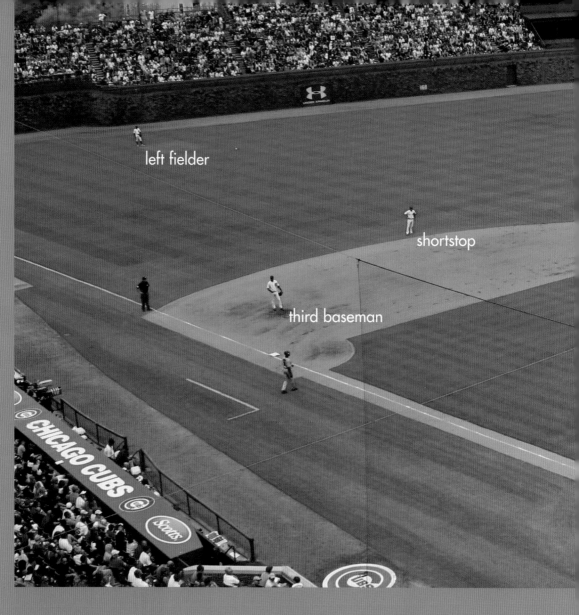

left fielder

shortstop

third baseman

What positions could I play?

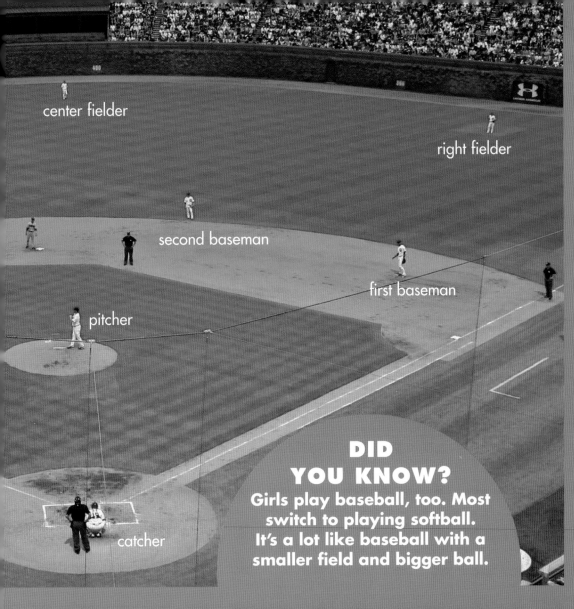

center fielder

right fielder

second baseman

first baseman

pitcher

catcher

DID YOU KNOW?
Girls play baseball, too. Most switch to playing softball. It's a lot like baseball with a smaller field and bigger ball.

The fielding team needs to fill nine spots. Outfielders catch fly balls. Infielders grab ground balls and throw quickly to get **outs**. The pitcher hurls the ball to the catcher. Coaches help you find your best position.

CHAPTER THREE

How do you score?

Teams score by getting **runs**. First, batters hit the ball. Then they run fast to first base. They may even get to second or third base. More hits keep the runners moving. When a runner makes it to **home plate**, the team scores a run. The team tries to score lots of runs before getting three outs.

A batter gets ready
to swing at a pitch.

How do you get outs?

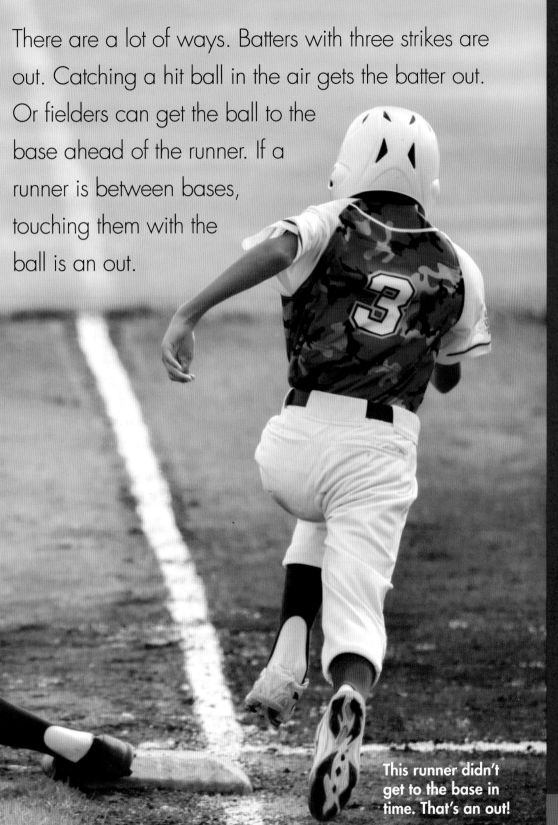

There are a lot of ways. Batters with three strikes are out. Catching a hit ball in the air gets the batter out. Or fielders can get the ball to the base ahead of the runner. If a runner is between bases, touching them with the ball is an out.

This runner didn't get to the base in time. That's an out!

What's the difference between a ball and a strike?

A pitch thrown in the **strike zone** is a strike. This zone is over home plate, but not too high or too low. A pitch outside of the strike zone is called a **ball**. An umpire calls the pitches. If a batter swings and misses, it is always a strike.

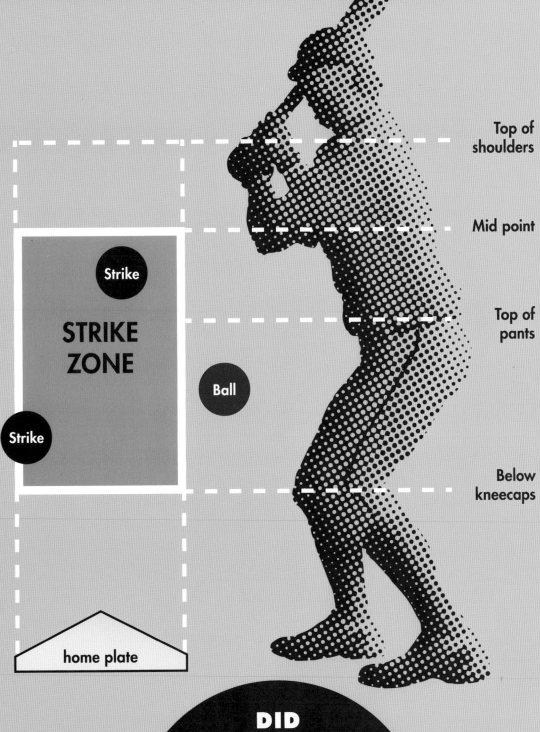

Top of
shoulders

Mid point

Top of
pants

Below
kneecaps

Strike

**STRIKE
ZONE**

Ball

Strike

home plate

**DID
YOU KNOW?**
3 strikes—strikeout,
batter is out
4 balls—walk,
batter goes to first base

A scoreboard shows the runs, innings, outs, and other game information.

HOME   INNING   GUEST

BALL   STRIKE   OUT   H-E

DID YOU KNOW?
If the score is tied, the game goes into extra innings. There is no limit to the number of extra innings. A game in 1981 lasted 33 innings!

How long is a game?

Players high five each other at the end of a game.

Baseball does not have a time clock. A game is measured in **innings**. Each team takes a turn hitting. After three outs, it's the other team's turn. That's an inning. Pro games are at least nine innings long. They take about three hours. Kids might play fewer innings.

Is the catcher using sign language?

Sort of. The catcher uses hand signs. These tell the pitcher what kind of pitch to throw. The catcher's hand can also show where the pitcher should throw it. The pitcher nods if he likes the pitch. If not, he shakes his head to ask for another sign.

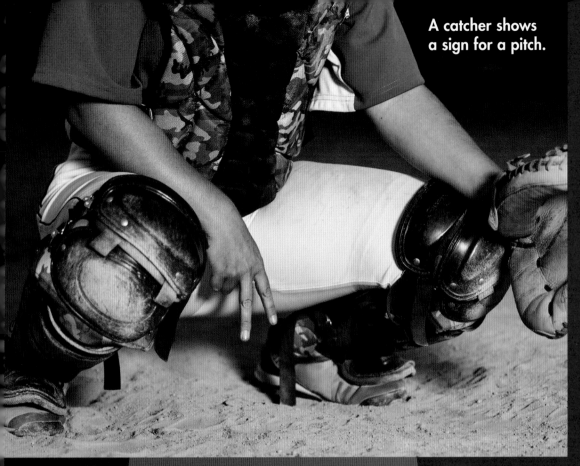

A catcher shows a sign for a pitch.

COMMON CATCHER SIGNS

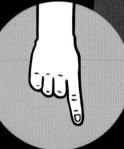

1 finger:
fastball

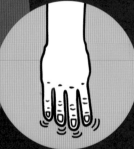

4 fingers, wiggling:
changeup

2 fingers:
curveball

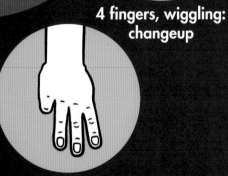

3 fingers:
slider

21

ASK MORE QUESTIONS

Why is a baseball game nine innings long?

Why does the pitcher stand on a mound?

Try a BIG QUESTION: Why is baseball called America's pastime?

SEARCH FOR ANSWERS

Search the library catalog or the Internet.
A librarian, teacher, or parent can help you.

Using Keywords
Find the looking glass.

Keywords are the most important words in your question.

?

If you want to know:

- why is a game nine innings, type: BASEBALL NINE INNINGS
- why the pitcher stands on a mound, type: PITCHER MOUND

FIND GOOD SOURCES

Here are some good, safe sources you can use in your research.
Your librarian can help you find more.

Books
I Can Be a Baseball Player
by Nancy Greenwood, 2021.

On the Baseball Team
by Stephane Hillard, 2022.

The Everything Kids' Baseball Book
11th Edition, by Jacobs Greg, 2020.

Internet Sites
Little League Baseball
https://www.littleleague.org/ play-little-league/baseball/
The official website for Little League Baseball has a lot of information, news, and rules.

Major League Baseball Kids
https://www.mlb.com/fans/kids
MLB's official site for kids includes tips on how to become a better player.

Every effort has been made to ensure that these websites are appropriate for children. However, because of the nature of the Internet, it is impossible to guarantee that these sites will remain active indefinitely or that their contents will not be altered.

SHARE AND TAKE ACTION

Play catch with a friend.
Throw each other ground balls and pop flies. You don't always need nine players to have some fun at the park.

Go to a high school or college game.
Watch how the players at each position play and work together.

Ask an older player for tips.
Find someone at school or ask an older family member.

GLOSSARY

ball A pitch outside the strike zone that the batter does not swing at.

home plate The five-sided base a runner must touch to score after running to all the bases. The batter stands by it when hitting.

infield The inner part of the field that includes the bases and home plate.

inning A part of a baseball game in which each team gets a turn at bat.

outfield The grassy area beyond the infield.

run A point scored when a runner reaches home plate after touching all the other bases.

strike A pitch the batter swings at and misses or that passes through the strike zone without the batter swinging.

strike zone The area over home plate, usually from the armpits to the knees of a batter, where the ball must be thrown to be a strike.

tee A straight pole a baseball is placed on for batting.

INDEX

About the Authors

Thomas K. and Heather Adamson are a husband-and-wife team who have written many books for kids. When they are not working, the couple likes to take hikes, watch movies, eat pizza, and of course, read. They live in South Dakota with their two sons and a Morkie dog named Moe.